李金元语录

李金元　凯文·麦康基　著

ACHIEVING YOUR DREAM

Words from Li Jinyuan

By Li Jinyuan, Kevin McConkey

壹嘉出版 1 PLUS BOOKS

成就梦想

前言

作为一名中国公民、企业家、慈善家，李金元先生行事低调，他将帮助他人获得健康、幸福和财富视为自己的责任，支持、帮助了世界各地的人们。

他追求人性的基本美德，他的领袖气质散发着独特的魅力，他对于全人类大家庭有着大爱。只要你听过他的讲话，你就会清楚地看到他是如何理解中国古代的传统文化和把握现代中国的发展方向，他透彻而充满力量的评论影响激励了很多的人。

出版这本书是为了将他的理念传播得更远，引导读者在自己的生活中进行反思并付诸实践。凯文·麦康基通过与他进行讨论和回顾他的演讲，以"健康"、"幸福"和"财富"作为关键词，总结提炼了他的人生感悟。这也是李金元先生所希望的。

Preface

Li Jinyuan, as a person, a businessman, a philanthropist and a citizen of China has assisted, guided, and supported many people around the world. He has done this quietly and without fanfare, believing it is his responsibility to help others to achieve health, happiness and fortune.

His deep belief in the essential goodness of people, his own charisma as a leader, his love for and commitment to all human beings and his understanding of the traditions of the ancient China and the direction of the modern China all become clear to people when they hear him speak. The clarity and the power of his comments have inspired many.

This collection of Li's thoughts is a way to take his voice further, and to do so in a way that readers can come back to for reflection and guidance in their own lives. Kevin McConkey obtained his thoughts through discussion and a review of Li's presentations and speeches. We have grouped the key words and thoughts under the broad categories of health, happiness and fortune because that is what Li Jinyuan wishes for all.

作者

Author

李金元毕业于南开大学。他是天狮集团的创始人，这是一家总部位于中华人民共和国天津市的民营企业。由于他的工作和对社会的贡献，他曾多次获得国际、国内奖项。本书包括一篇他的简短传记。

Li Jinyuan is a graduate of Nankai University. He is founder and Chairman of Tiens Group Co. Limited, a private company headquarted in Tianjin, People's Republic of China. He has received awards and honors within China and from around the world for his work and his contributions to the society. A brief biography of Li is included in this book.

李金元　Li Jinyuan

作者

Author

凱文·麦康基 Kevin McConkey

　　凯文·麦康基毕业于澳大利亚昆士兰大学，是新南威尔士大学心理学荣誉教授。他是天狮集团的国际顾问。他曾获得多种奖项和荣誉，包括澳大利亚社会科学院研究员，澳大利亚公司董事协会成员，以及澳大利亚勋章。

Kevin McConkey is a graduate of the University of Queensland and is an Emeritus Professor of Psychology at the University of New South Wales, Australia. He is an International Advisor to Tiens Group. He has received awards and honors within Australia, including being a Fellow of the Academy of the Social Sciences in Australia, a Fellow of the Australian Institute of Company Directors, and a Member of the Order of Australia.

致谢
Acknowledgments

我们非常感谢李金元先生与我们讨论并分享他的想法。我们也要感谢张可、杨学哲和李至斌的协助，帮助我们整理汇编李金元先生在演讲文稿和会议报告中的精彩论点与思想火花，感谢克里斯多夫·希迪准备传记摘要并审校英文，感谢尉明辉、杨学哲、李至斌、路茜、刘玉莹和张艳菁准备和审校中文，还要特别感谢阎玉鹏和路茜的协调配合。我们还感谢视觉共振设计工作室提供设计和插图，以及壹嘉出版和咨询公司的刘雁对出版物的整体编校和协调。

We are grateful to Li Zhibin, Yang Xuezhe and Zhang Kee for assistance in finding Li's comments in speeches and presentations, to Christopher Sheedy for preparing the brief biography and for reviewing English language expressions, and to Li Zhibin, Liu Yuying, Lu Xi, Wei Minghui, Yang Xuezhe, Michael Yu and Zhang Yanjing for preparing and reviewing Chinese language expressions. We give very special thanks also to Lu Xi and to Yan Yupeng for overall coordination and strong support.

We are grateful also to PanGoVision for design and illustration, and to Liu Yan of 1 Plus Publishing and Consulting for editorial review and coordination of publication.

李金元小传

克里斯多夫·希迪

他以超凡的想象力创造了世界上最大的聚焦大健康产业的跨国集团之一。他白手起家，如今公司已经发展成为业务遍及190多个国家和地区，赢得4000多万家庭消费者信赖的跨国集团。亿万富豪企业家李金元先生以其独到的商业模式，激发了全球千千万万的创业灵感，带来事业机会。他的财富历程充满了坚定的决心，他的事业成功基于对人性的深刻理解与精准把握。这些独到的见解，使得李金元先生能够广泛汇聚他人参与到他的事业梦想。

Christopher Sheedy

Brief Biography of

Li Jinyuan

One man imagined and created one of the world's largest health-focused organizations. On his own he built the company, from the ground up, into what is now an esteemed multinational with over 40 million customers in 190 countries. Now an inspiration to thousands globally, billionaire entrepreneur Li Jinyuan found his own way in the business world, his journey fueled by pure determination and his success reliant on a deep and innate understanding of the human nature. This understanding offered him the power to engage others in his dream.

成功的道路并不平坦，但企业家要获得成功没有其他道路，只有持续地奋斗。他的奋斗在他还是个大男孩的时候就已经开始，他成长于毛泽东时代的中国农村，他相信他注定会做出一番与众不同的大事业，尽管当时他并不明确知道这要如何实现。他渴望接受教育，但他还是在 14 岁时选择离开学校，在社会这所大学里继续学习成长。

他的第一份工作，是在国有企业从事石油开采，李金元先生的创业之火即将点燃。他回忆道："我花了几年时间，随工程队在中国各地开采石油。""但后来我被调到了行政后勤工作。我的工作是帮助改善工友的生活，我开始在中国各地采购商品。"

故事从一卡车油的贸易交换开始，通常他会把油运到沿海地区，交易新鲜捕获的鱼。有时候就运回鱼，或者有时候将鱼交易成面粉，面粉交易啤酒，啤酒交易自行车等。每次他带回的货物价值都比运出去的油价值高。这个年轻的采购谈判专家越来越得心应手。而事实证明，李金元先生非常擅长这项工作。

几年之后，他开始了自己的生意，在自由市场上开展贸易，积累了人生的第一桶金，并用这些资金在他的家乡河北省沧州周边兴建了几家工厂——面粉厂、塑料厂、蛋白粉厂，而这些只是他事业的刚刚起步。

The path to success was not smooth and was characterised by struggle, but the entrepreneur would have it no other way. The journey, he says, began when he was a young boy growing up in a rural village during Mao Zedong's era in China. Even then Li knew that he was born to make a difference, but at the time he wasn't sure how. Although he had a great passion for education, he chose to leave school at 14 and instead do his learning out in the world.

During his very first job, prospecting for oil with a state-owned business, Li's entrepreneurial flair became immediately apparent. "I spent a few years traveling around China with a team, drilling for oil," he recalls. "But then I was offered a role in human resources. My job was to help improve the lives of the company's staff, so I began trading goods between various regions in China."

He'd begin with a truckload of oil, which he typically took to the coast and traded for freshly caught fish. The trade might end there, or the fish could be traded for flour, and the flour for beer, and the beer for bicycles, and so on, as long as he returned with more than he left with. The young negotiator was doing his job. And as it turned out, Li was very good at this job.

He turned it into his own business several years later, trading goods on the open market and earning a small fortune, which he used to build several factories near his hometown of Cangzhou in Hebei Province. These busi-

后来，李金元先生意识到一个新的市场机遇，那就是创造一个直接利于广大消费者健康的产业（如李金元先生所说，生活失去健康，就等于地球没有太阳）。天狮集团应运而生，他的第一款产品是骨骼强化营养配方的高钙素（目前仍然是天狮最畅销的拳头产品）。

伴随他深爱的中国经济飞速发展，他的事业版图也迅猛扩张。然而，李金元先生从来没有忘记他对教育事业的热情，也从没忘记他要改变世界的初心，所以在他刚刚有能力付诸行动的时候，他就毅然在自己的家乡沧州，为当地的孩子们修建了两所全新的学校，改善当地教育条件。此后，他在中国和世界各地，资助援建了超过 100 所学校。

随着天狮集团的事业改善全球数千万家庭的健康水平并提升生活质量，李金元先生还将其业务版图延伸至教育事业。他创建了招收 6000 名学生规模的天狮学院，这是目前天津唯一的私立本科高等教育机构。2017 年，李金元先生的教育梦想将再次升级，他将兴建一所可容纳 30000 名学生的新的大学校园。

一路走来，李金元先生不断将财富与众多全心支持天狮事业的人们分享。截至目前，李金元先生及天狮集团在教育、医疗、灾害救助、公益组织、慈善机构、扶贫项目等方面资助的爱心款物超过 15 亿元人民币(超过 2.3 亿美元)，李金元先生也因热衷慈善事业而闻名。

nesses produced flour, plastic parts and protein products, but he was just getting started.

Li recognized a new opportunity to create a business that would directly benefit the health of its customers (life without health, Li says, "is equal to the earth without the sun"). The Tiens Group was born, its first product (and presently still its best seller) a bone-strengthening nutritional formula known as Super Calcium Powder.

As the fortunes of his beloved China grew, so did those of his business. But Li never forgot his original passion for education or his desire to make a difference in the world. As soon as he was able, he travelled back to his hometown of Cangzhou and built for the local children two new schools. Since then he has funded the building of over 100 schools in China and elsewhere.

As Tiens Group began to have a positive effect on the health of ten millions of people around the globe, Li also directed the business into the realm of education. He launched Tianshi College, a 6000-student facility that is Tianjin's only private, higher-education institution. In 2017, Li's education dream took another leap forward with the development of a new university campus capable of educating 30,000 students annually.

Along the way Li shared his wealth amongst those who supported causes close to his heart. Now famous for their philanthropy, Li and the Tiens Group have so far

"想象如何改善人们的生活，是我童年最美好的记忆。"李金元先生说，"如今我有能力付诸实施，这就是我梦想的实现。"

　　"每当我看到人们痛苦、饥饿的时候，我感同身受。当我还是孩子的时候，我就曾把我的饼干分发给穷苦的小伙伴，因为当我看到他们的苦难，我的心里就感到非常的沉重，因此每个月我都向穷困的人分发饼干。"

　　"我的美好记忆都是关于自我激励，坚信我可以改变世界让其更美好，而我不好的回忆都是来源于他人的痛苦。创办企业的经历，让我能在改善别人的生活上发挥更大的作用。"

　　李金元先生对人性的驱动力的独特见解，从幸福到遗憾，从参与到冷漠，从胜利到悲观，都为他非凡的成功提供了动力。在这本书中，李金元先生分享了他近半个世纪的商业和慈善成就所获得的智慧、知识和经验，希望您有所收获。

　　只要你相信，他说，你就会获得幸福，感恩和希望。别无他途。

given away over 1.5 billion RMB (over USD $230 million) to schools and hospitals, disaster relief funds and charities, needy individuals and families.

"My best memories from childhood were the times I spent imagining how I could be able to improve people's lives," he says. "Now I am able to do that, and it is the fulfillment of my dream."

"I saw people suffering and I saw people starving. As a child, when I had cookies I gave them away to poor people because when I saw people suffering like that it became a psychological burden for me. Each month I tried to distribute some cookies to poor people."

"So my good memories were about self-motivation, thinking that I could change things. My bad memories came from seeing the suffering of others. My entrepreneurial journey has made it possible for me to make a difference on a greater scale."

Li's extraordinary insights into the drivers of human nature, from happiness to regret, from engagement to apathy, and from triumph to tragedy have powered his phenomenal success. For your enjoyment, in this book Li shares that wisdom, knowledge and experience gained over almost half a century of business and philanthropic accomplishment.

"If you believe," he says, "you will achieve happiness, gratitude and hope. Nothing else matters."

文化 Culture 34	家 Home 35	爱 Love 36	幸 福
孩子 Children 37	快乐 Happiness 39	和谐 Harmony 40	HAPPINESS

沟通 Communication 41	同情心 Compassion 42

感恩 Gratitude 43	家庭 Family 44	改变 Change 45
独处 Alone 46	希望 Hope 48	助人 Help 49

欲望 Desire 50	遗憾 Regret 51

仪式 Ceremony 52	谅解 Forgiveness 53	平凡 Ordinary 54
妥协 Compromise 55	慈善 Charity 55	目标 Goal 56

晚年幸福 Happiness When Old 59	牺牲 Sacrifice 60

年轻人 The Young 61	悔恨 Hate 62	自私 Selfishness 63
海洋 Ocean 64	慷慨 Generous 65	马 Horse 67

		尊重 Respect 70	创新 Innovation 71	贫穷 Poverty 72
财富 FORTUNE		能量 Power 73	逆境 Adversity 74	金钱 Money 75
		成功 Success 76	努力 Effort 77	
		命运 Fate 78	勇敢 Bravery 78	挑战 Challenge 79
		财富 Wealth 80	团队 Team 81	领导力 Leadership 81
		历史 History 82	决定 Decision 84	腐败 Corruption 85
		龙 Dragon 86	动力 Motivation 87	前进 Advance 88

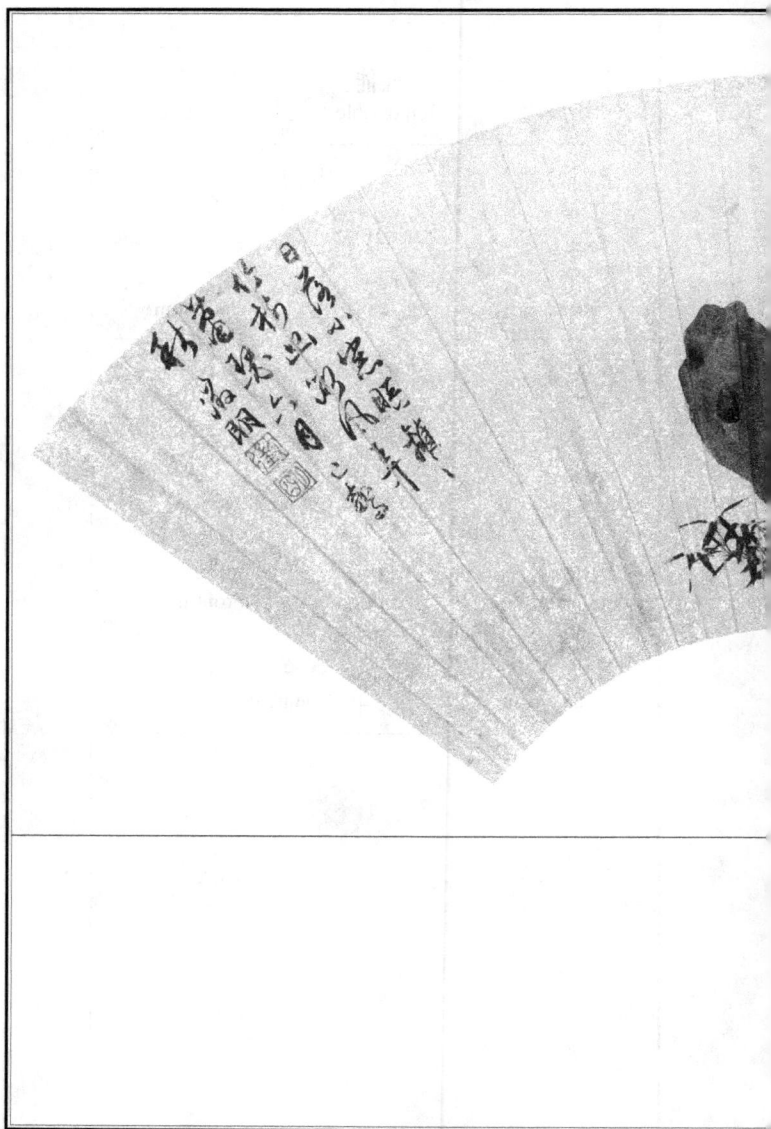

Ming Dynasty
Wen Zhengming
Cypress, Bamboo and Rock

Wen Zhengming was a representative of
the Wu genre of Ming Dynasty. He has a
clear and elegant style that resonates with
the long history of the Chinese tradition.

《古柏竹石图》 ◎ 明 ◎ 文征明

文征明是明代吴派的代表画家，
风格清雅秀丽。

第一部

健康

I

HEALTH

力量

感恩令人强大有力。如果你的周遭没有爱，你也不能给予爱，你就是个失败者。有了爱和感恩这样的积极力量，才能有积极的态度，引领你走向完美与强大。

STRENGTH

You are strong and healthy when you are grateful. When there is no love around you and when you don't give love to others, you lose. When you have this true element of love and gratitude, you gain more and more strength. These are positive forces which lead to the perfect positive attitude of strength and health.

睡眠

坦诚的心和良好的睡眠让我们能更好地面对困难，应对生活的挑战，享受生活中的美好时光。积极的态度和良好的睡眠是帮助你恢复的最好途径。当你醒来的时候，你会有更好的态度去面对世界，充满活力地前行。

SLEEP

An open heart and good sleep allow us to face difficulties, to have capacity to deal with the challenges of life and to better enjoy the good times of life. A positive attitude and a good sleep are the best ways to recover from a life challenge. When you wake up you have a better attitude to face the world, and to be dynamic in moving forward.

6

老年

在中国，六十岁是生命中的一个重要节点，既是迈向老年，也是新生，因为你正在跳转到生命的下一个周期（新的甲子）。你的心态应当回到初始。在许多方面，你再次年轻，有很多机会。所以「老年」亦是一个全新的开始。

OLD

In China, 60 years of age is an important step in life. It is old but also young because you are now jumping to the next cycle of life. So your mentality comes back to the beginning. In many ways you are young again, with many opportunities. So 'old' is a new beginning.

安康

幸福对我们所有人都是必不可少的，健康的个体则是社会进步的必要条件。如果人们不健康，社会就不能前进。健康对于我一直是头等大事，不仅因为我从事医疗保健行业，更因为健康是个人和社会进步的重要基石。

WELLBEING

Wellbeing is essential for all of us, but the healthy person is also essential for the social progress. If people are not well, the society cannot move forward. Health is always my number one priority, not only because I am in the healthcare business, but also because health is the essential building block for individual and social progress.

诚实

健康的人应该是一名诚实的人，不诚实是不健康的。我们都需要诚实地面对自己，真实地了解自己。然后，我们要对他人敞开心扉，不要对他人有任何的欺瞒。诚实会带来尊重和身心的健康幸福。如果别人不诚实，我们也许很难做到诚心以对，但要让你自己超乎于那些不诚实的人之上。

HONESTY

A healthy person is an honest person. Being dishonest is unhealthy. We all need to be honest first with ourselves, to understand ourselves. Then we need to be open with others, and open to others, to not hide anything. Honesty will bring respect and a sense of wellbeing. It can sometimes be difficult to be honest if others are not, but always lift yourself above those who do not have the value of honesty.

9

出生

出生是独立个体生命的开始。人们赤条条来，赤条条去，但在生死之间，人是有使命的。使命有时是由人自己定义，有时是由他人定义。有人生来即肩负使命，有人却生活得毫无目标，浑浑噩噩。健康的人会努力寻找使命、目标，获得对生命的理解。

BIRTH

Birth is the beginning of an independent life. People are born with nothing and will pass away with nothing. But in between, people have a mission, which is sometimes defined by themselves and sometimes by others. Some people are born to develop a mission, while others are born but never have or develop a mission or a purpose – they fill in time without reason between birth and death. Healthy people strive to find their mission, their purpose, their understanding of life.

沧州铁狮 ◎ 现代

铁狮气势恢宏，目光炯炯，似乎在为他的群

体守望，古朴高大的形象诠释了坚毅、威

猛、正义的王者气度。

Modern
Cangzhou's Iron lion

The iron lion's eye is fixed
on something, as if he is
guarding his community,
the simple and tall image
signifies fortitude, fierceness
and the bearing of a king.

狮子

狮子是百兽之王，是勇气和力量的象征。狮王是领导者、提供者、保护者，它的威严令人敬畏。

LION

The lion is the king of animals and the symbol of courage and strength. The lion is the leader, the provider, the protector and the one that promotes the pride of the community.

長洲文徵明寫像

《老子像》◎ 明 ◎ 文徵明

文徵明是明代大家，诗文书画无一不精。他的老子像，细腻严谨，气度沉静。

Ming Dynasty, Wen Zhengming, **Lao Tsu**
149 × 24cm

Wen Zhengming was famous for his poems, essays, calligraphy and paintings. This painting shows great scrupulousness and tranquility inside.

智慧

有智慧的人生是勇敢的人生。智慧带来适应力、人际关系技巧和对周围环境和周围人的理解。但只有智慧本身是不够的，将智慧与勇气，人际关系技巧和战略眼光结合在一起，才是非凡而强大的。

WISDOM

Life with wisdom is a bold life. Wisdom brings resilience, interpersonal skills and an understanding of your environment and the people around you. But wisdom on its own is not enough. Boldness, interpersonal skills and strategic vision, if combined with wisdom, are very powerful.

死亡

死亡是生命中不可回避的一部分，不可怕也不值得担心。但我们应该思考我们死后会留下什么。有些人为后代留下了丰富遗产，有些人除了孩子，没有留下任何遗产。我们都应该尽力为我们的后辈留下宝贵的遗产。

DEATH

Death is a natural part of life, not to be feared and not to be concerned about. But we should think about what we will leave when we die. Some people pass away with an important legacy for the following generations. Others just pass away without leaving any legacy, other than perhaps the birth of children. We should all try to leave a legacy of good for those who follow us.

抑郁

压力感、个人压力、社会压力、工作压力、无助感、无法应付压力都会导致短期或长期的抑郁。重要的是不管是孩子还是成年人，都要学会面对压力，进而避免沮丧的情绪。

DEPRESSION

A sense of pressure, personal pressure, social pressure, work pressure, a feeling of being helpless, of not being able to deal with the pressure can all lead to depression for a short or long time. What is important is that we learn as children and as adults how to handle the pressures that we face, and then we can avoid much of a feeling of depression.

威胁

生命中最大的威胁不是疾病，而是不能保持身体健康。健康是人类最大的财富。如果失去健康，相当于地球没有太阳。我致力于人类的健康事业，我们用勤劳的双手托起生命的太阳。

THREAT

The biggest threat to our life is not disease, but rather not keeping in good health. Health is the greatest wealth of mankind. If we are not healthy, then it is equal to the earth without the sun. I am committed to the cause of human health, and we should all use hard-working hands to hold up the sun of life.

世界

在这个时代，我们每个人都应该具备世界眼光。用世界眼光来看待自己，理解我们在世界上的位置和贡献，同时保持好奇心，对于不同事物乐于去学习和理解，并尽力帮助我们的社区、我们的国家和我们的世界，这是精神健康的一部分。

WORLD

In these times, we should all take a world view and try to understand our place and contribution in the world. It is part of being mentally healthy to take an interest in different things, to continue to learn and understand, and to do what we can, whether small or large, to help our community, country and world.

骄傲

我们应该为自己的成就感到骄傲，但不要太骄傲，因为过于骄傲会使我们变得心胸狭隘，这对心灵的健康无益。值得我们为之骄傲的是我们能够以我们的方式帮助他人，同时，我们也应该为得到他人的帮助而骄傲和感激，这才是衡量健康生活方式的真正标准。我最大的骄傲是，我能感受到爱，创造爱和传播爱。

PRIDE

We should be proud of our achievements, but not too proud because being too proud will make us narrow and unhealthy in mind and heart. We should be proud of the ways in which we can help others, since doing something for others is much better than doing things for yourself. And we should be proud and grateful, when others help us because that is the true measure of a healthy relationship. My biggest pride happens when I feel love, create love and spread love.

食物

食物是健康生活的基本燃料。正确的食物带来正确的生活态度，给生命以活力。错误的食物会导致消极的思想和感受，导致思想和身体上的疾病。我们必须明白食物的重要性，并努力选择有助于让我们不断进步、成长的食物。

FOOD

Food is the essential fuel of a healthy life. The right food creates the right attitude of life and gives the energy for life. The wrong food can lead to negative thoughts and feelings, and to sickness in mind and body. We must all understand the importance of food and strive to choose the food that makes us better people.

环境

无论居住或工作，你都需要一个良好和健康的环境。健康的环境能帮助你保持身体的健康，帮助你建立和维护良好的人际关系，更有效率地工作，更好地享受生活。

我们都是环境的一部分，我们必须承担自己的责任，改善环境，使其可持续发展，而不能破坏环境，那是将来会后悔的事情。环境也是我们留给子孙后代的遗产。我们必须努力保护好这份遗产并并移交给他们。

ENVIRONMENT

Wherever you live or work, you need a good and healthy environment. You need one that helps you to be healthy, that helps you talk and meet with other people, that helps you do enjoyable and productive things. We are all part of the environment and we all have to take some responsibility for making it as good as we can and influencing it positively. We also have to look to the future and make the environment sustainable to ensure that we do not do things now that we will regret in the future. The environment is a legacy we pass to the future generations. We must work to make that legacy a good one for them.

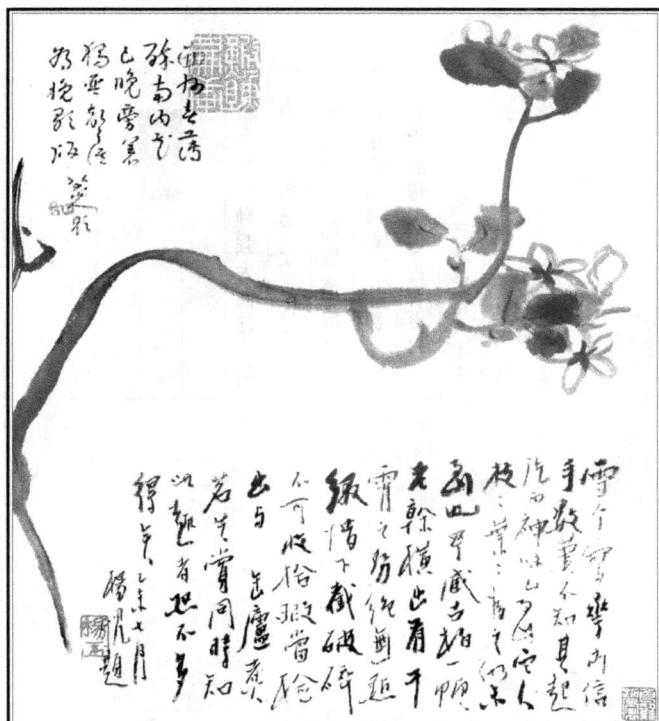

Qing Dynasty
Bada Shanren
Jasmine

31.5 × 28cm
Bada Shanren's art transforms
from figural to abstract, and
from traditional to modern.

八大山人的艺术表现出从具象到抽象，
从传统到现代的鲜明特点。

《茉莉花图》◎ 清 ◎ 八大山人

信念

信念是一种强大而健康的力量。信念是你对目标的承诺，是你做事的动力和信心的源泉。你需要检查你的信念是否有良好基础，错误的理念会把人引入歧路。信仰会带来信心，帮你、也帮助你生活中的其他人获得成就。

BELIEF

Belief is a powerful and healthy force. It is your commitment to a goal. Belief is the source of motivation and of confidence in what you are doing. You need to check that your belief has a good basis and is not something that will lead you to do wrong things. Belief feeds the confidence you need to achieve good things in your own life and in the lives of others.

坚韧

这是我们忍耐和坚持的能力。有些人很有韧性，但有些人不是。在生活中保持一个明确的目标，你就会有韧性，你会充满希望地努力实现目标，不会被不相关的事情所打扰。

RESILIENCE

This is our capacity to endure and persist. Some people are very resilient but others are not. People can become resilient by having a clear goal in life and by keeping hope and effort on that goal, and by not being distracted by the things that interfere with that goal.

责任

有责任感是一种健康的状态。人应该有梦想，懂得感恩。而梦想和感恩创造了责任感，让我们走向成功和懂得回报社会。在我年轻的时候，当我看到穷人我会感同身受非常难过，我尽力去帮助他们。当我长大了，我意识到我的事业可以帮助实现我童年的梦想。

RESPONSIBILITY

It is healthy to be responsible and accountable. I have a dream in life and I know how to be grateful. Together, a dream and gratitude create a sense of responsibility to achieve and to give back. When I was young, my heart felt very sad when I saw poor people and I tried to do things to help them. When I grew up, I realized that my business could achieve my childhood's dream.

随着我的生意越来越大，我开始捐款来帮助人们。但后来我意识到，捐钱并不是唯一的帮助方式。更重要的是要倡导更多的人参与对社会的共同承诺，承担帮助他人的责任。这就是我不断追求的。我认为，财富越多，帮助别人的责任就越大。

As my business became bigger and bigger I understood that I could give donations to help people and communities. But then I realized that giving money is not the only way to help. Rather, it is important to convince more people to become involved in the common commitment to society, to take the responsibility of helping others. That is what I continue to pursue. I think the greater the wealth, the greater the responsibility to help others in many different ways.

恐惧

恐惧主要是对自己缺乏信心，或对自己处理不同情况的能力缺乏信心。如何克服恐惧？你要全神贯注于你的梦想，始终清楚地知道你的目标是什么，并努力获得他人的支持。当你有一个真正的梦想，并且努力为之奋斗，而且你懂得感恩，那么，你也就有了自信。梦想、感恩、责任和使命感会让你远离恐惧，使你成为一个身心健康、胸襟开阔、意志坚强的人。

FEAR

Fear is mostly a lack of confidence in yourself or your ability to deal with different situations. You overcome fear by keeping focus on your dream, by getting support from others, by being very clear about your dream and your goal. When you really have a true goal to which you are committed, and you know how to be grateful, then you know how to be confident. The dream, the gratitude, the responsibility and the sense of mission keep fear away. These things make you a healthy person with an open and strong heart.

衰老

衰老是一个自然循环的过程。你不可能对抗这个循环。但无论你身处这个循环中的哪个位置，你都可以找到你的健康和福祉。坚实的经济基础，良师益友，目标感，会在你年老的时候给你一个安身立命之地，也会让你有条件去帮助处于这个循环中不同位置的他人。

AGING

Aging is a natural cycle. You cannot fight this cycle, but you can find your place of health and wellbeing wherever you are in this cycle. Enough money, good friends and a sense of purpose will give you a good place in the cycle as you age. They will also allow you to help others at different places in the cycle.

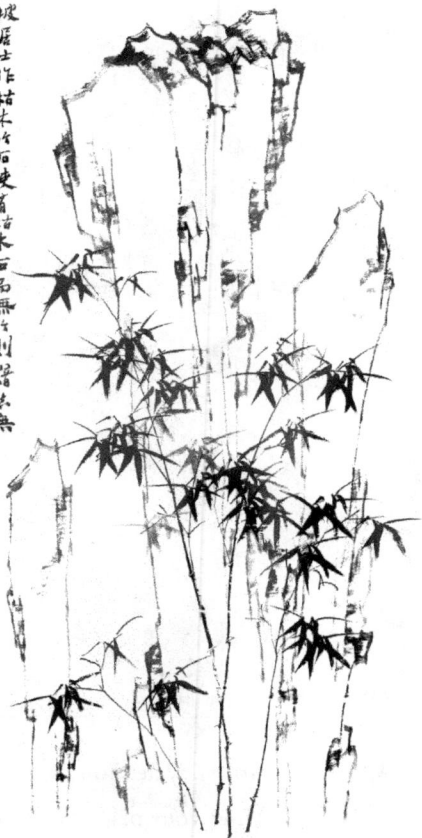

《竹石图轴》◎ 清 ◎ 郑板桥

郑板桥一生只画竹、兰、石，这是他的代表作之一。在中国传统文化中，竹代表正直，兰代表高洁，石代表坚定。

Qing Dynasty, Zheng Banqiao, **Bamboo and Rock**
217.4 × 120.6cm

Zheng Banqiao painted only bamboo, orchid and rocks in his whole life. In Chinese culture, bamboo represents integrity, orchid represents elegance and rock represents steadyfast.

二百年后

我希望两百年后，人们依然记得我的名字，他们会说，这个人帮助很多人提高了生活水平，改善了健康状况，并且帮助他们实现了人生目标。

IN 200 YEARS

I hope that in 200 years, when they remember my name, people will say that I helped to improve standards of life, health and many generations achieve their goals in life.

给孩子的箴言

人要有目标、有梦想。我鼓励孩子们做梦，给自己设定目标。更重要的是，要制定计划来实现目标。要让梦想成真，还要不断地对计划进行调整、改进、革新。要做自我评估和自我批评。要学习知识，并能够运用。我会告诉孩子，只要你制定计划，不断学习，不断努力去实现，一切都是可能的。最后，还要有一颗开放、感恩的心，和好朋友们。

ADVICE TO CHILD

I encourage a child to have a goal and a dream in life. However, I strongly advise that he or she also develops a plan for how to achieve that goal. To achieve a dream you need a plan that you keep adjusting and improving and innovating all the time. You have to do self-assessment and self-criticism all the time. You have to get more knowledge, learn more and apply that new knowledge. I would tell the child that anything is possible with a goal, a plan, knowledge and effort. Wrap those things with an open heart, gratitude and dear friends.

教育

我年轻的时候曾盼着我们的村子有所好学校。那时我就意识到，教育能带来改变，改变我们村子以及村民的未来。教育是通向美好未来的唯一途径，教育是国家繁荣发展的基石，也是个人成功和幸福的基础。服务国家、回报社会的最佳途径就是促进教育事业的发展。

EDUCATION

When I was young I wanted a good school in my village. Even then I knew education means change. It meant a future for the people of my village. Education is the only way to find a better future. The best way to serve a country and give back to society is to promote the development of education. Education is the foundation of national prosperity and development, as well as individual prosperity and happiness. Education and knowledge are the real health and wealth of people and countries.

第二部

幸福

II

HAPPINESS

文化

文化有很多种含义。它可以是你的个人修养和教育，它可能是一种文明和一个社会的行为方式，以及一个国家的价值观。这两种理解都至关重要，而且会随着时间的推移和社会的进步而改变。我们都应努力去发现和发展那些有益于我们和社会的文化、价值观以及行为方式。

CULTURE

Culture has many meanings. It can be your personal cultivation and education, leading to a better understanding of your place in the world. It could be the way that a civilization and a society behave, and the things that are valued in a country. Both of these meanings of culture are important, and both change over time and over different societies. We should all try to find and develop the culture, the values and the behaviors that are good for us and for the society in which we live.

家

家是幸福所在，其中很重要的一部分是家庭成员对彼此的尊重，尤其是对长辈。中国文化博大精深，但最基本的就是孝敬父母。懂得尊重和感恩才能为家庭贡献力量。不懂感恩，便无法谈及回报家庭乃至奉献社会。如果父母孝敬自己的长辈，言传身教之下，孩子们也会耳濡目染。这便是通过尊重和感恩来营造幸福家庭的方法。

HOME

Happiness can be found in the home, and an important part of that is the respect that family members show to each other, especially the elders. In the Chinese culture the respect of parents is essential. To be able to contribute in the home you need to be respectful and grateful. If you don't know how to be grateful you cannot contribute to your family or to society. When children see parents being respectful to their own parents, then those children will learn. This is the way to create a happy home through respect and gratitude to all.

爱

就像父母对孩子无私的爱，我们爱自己的父母和家人也都应不求回报。抚养和教育孩子时理应如此。在中国，「爱」有很多深刻的含义，包括对家庭的爱，对社会和国家的爱。没有「大家」哪有「小家」。感恩是创造爱的一个重要组成部分，生活因感恩而美好。

LOVE

Love your parents and love your family without asking something in return, because the love that parents have for their children does not involve asking anything in return. That is how you raise your children and how you help them to learn. Love in China has a lot of very deep meanings. You love your family, you love society as a whole and you love your country. Without a 'big family' you can never have a 'small family'. Being grateful is a very important part of love. If we are all grateful to each other, then life is perfect.

孩子

孩子是祖国的未来和幸福的源泉。在毛泽东主席领导下，中国走上现代化发展道路，激发了人民的自豪感；随着邓小平同志改革开放政策的提出，人们开始积极创业，塑造未来。这一改革进程持续了很长时间。孩子是祖国的未来和希望，所以教育至关重要。接受良好教育的人决定国家的未来，未接受教育的孩子，将会成为国家的负担。孩子是民族未来的希望，关键在于教育。

CHILDREN

Children are the future and the happiness of China. When Chairman Mao Zedong created the development process of modern China, the people began to gain pride. With the economic reform of Deng Xiaoping, people began to be motivated to create businesses, which helped shape our future. These processes took a lot of time. Generation after generation contributed. Children always were and always will be the future of China, our new page. That's why education is so important for children. Educated people are the future of this country. Children who are not educated will become a burden for the country. Children are the hope of the future, and the child's wish is education.

《荷花翠鸟图》◎ 清 ◎ 八大山人

作为明朝皇室宗亲，生活在满清统治之下的八大山人以遁世和孤傲的姿态表达自我。他的画便是他的心志的写真。

Qing Dynasty, Bada Shanren, **Lotus and Bird**
121 × 66cm

As a royal member of the Ming Dynasty, Bada Shanren chose to escape from the Qing Dynasty to live in remote temples and to live in a proud way. His paintings show the views of the world from this perspective.

快乐

快乐与欲望息息相关。简约的生活欲望很容易让人知足常乐，追求的过多，便很难得到快乐，因为总有一些事情是遥不可及的。对于我来说，快乐很简单。因为我总是尽力去帮助别人，这是我真正快乐的源泉。

HAPPINESS

Happiness is linked to desire. If you don't desire many things, then you can be happy very easily. If you desire many things, then it may be harder for you to be happy in life, because there is always something even further out of reach. For me, it is very simple. I always try my best to help others, because this is where I find my real happiness.

和谐

我们都向往和追求和谐：这样才能舒适而温馨地生活、工作，获得共同进步。和谐是建立在互相信任的基础上，并能带给我们成功与幸福。团结协作，和谐共处。合作的力量是无法抗拒的，它存在于人类生活、爱情和工作的方方面面。

HARMONY

We all look for harmony, for the comfort and the warmth of living and working and moving forward together. When people trust each other they will find harmony. That harmony will bring success and happiness. Teamwork and harmony create being together, and being together creates teamwork and harmony. Being together can be an unstoppable force in life, in love, in work and in all things that matter to us as human beings.

沟通

成功的沟通是真心换真心，

真情换真情，真爱换真爱。

良好的沟通可以弥合人与社

会之间的很多认识鸿沟。通

过沟通和语言技巧来展示一

个人的思维方式以及诚信和

态度。我们都应善于倾听，

理性思考，并开诚布公地尽

情表达自己。

COMMUNICATION

Successful communication is heart to heart, truth for truth and love for love. Good communication can bridge many gaps between people and societies. Communication and language skills show how a person thinks and the honesty and attitude of the person. We should all try to be good at listening, rational thinking and expressing ourselves in an open way.

同情心

施展同情心要根据情况而定。毫无能力、时运不济的弱势群体值得同情，有些人的无心之过可以怜悯。感同身受，怀有同情心有时是好事，但同情心不能泛滥，如果是因为自作自受而身处困境，那便不值得同情。

COMPASSION

Depending on the situation, compassion should be shown or maybe not shown. You can show compassion for people who are weaker than you and have not had opportunities, and you can feel for them. Or for people who have made an unintentional mistake and you feel their pain. Sometimes it is good to have compassion. Sometimes though, compassion should not happen, even when the other person is in a bad situation, especially if they have made that situation themselves.

感恩

感恩是人类的基本原则。感
恩是做好事的动力源泉，也
是快乐的本质。人们必须要
学会感恩。感恩也意味着回
报父母和奉献社会。滴水之
恩当涌泉相报，这才是我们
要表达的感恩和要寻找到的
真正快乐。

GRATITUDE

To be grateful is a basic human principle. To be grateful can be a motivation, can be a force to do good in the world, and can be the essence of happiness. Human beings must learn to be grateful. Being grateful also means giving something in return – giving back to parents or to society. If you have small water given to you, then you should give back the whole river. That is showing gratitude and that is finding true happiness.

家庭，包括你的原生家庭和你与别人一起创建的家庭，子孙后代创建的家庭，都是命运的一部分，创造幸福的一部分。家庭是我们的传承和珍宝，它决定了你在人类历史中的地位。

家庭

FAMILY

Family is part of destiny, part of happiness, including the family you come from, the family you create with others and the families that they then create. Families are our heritage and our legacy. Families place you in the history of human life.

改变

根据你在各个阶段的生活和
需要承担的责任，人们应该
时刻改变，学习新知识，挑
战新事物。生活就是要不断
成长、挑战、探索和创造，
在探索和成就中感受幸福。

CHANGE

Depending on the stage of your life and on your responsibilities, people should be changing, learning something new, doing something they have not done before, all the time. Life is about growth, about change, about exploring and about achievement. Happiness is found in these essential human activities.

独处

对这个词语，不同的人会有不同的理解。但每当我独自一人时，我感到安宁、舒适和平静。我希望别人也如此。

ALONE

This is a big word that has many meanings. But when I'm alone, I feel at peace. I feel comfortable and peaceful. I hope others do too.

《独立睥睨图》◎清 ◎ 八大山人

八大山人笔下的动物，都有一双桀骜不驯的眼睛。

Qing Dynasty
Bada Shanren
Standing Alone Looking Askance

110×74.5cm
All of the animals in Bada Shanren's paintings have eyes
that show great pride and unwavering focus.

希望

希望是一种梦想，是生活中寻找幸福的动力。当你陷入逆境，唯一陪伴你的，就是希望。希望、专注和努力能帮你渡过难关，但希望是其中最重要的因素。相信希望，相信自己，努力工作。

HOPE

Hope is a dream, a motivation in life to find happiness. Sometimes all you have in life, in difficult times, is hope. Hope, focus and effort can get you through those times, and hope is the most important factor. Believe in hope, believe in yourself and work hard.

助人

做对别人有帮助的人，愿意
考虑公众利益并为之行动，
同时心存感恩，时刻对别人
保有爱心。如果你不相信这
是一个充满爱的世界，你的
生活也会在沮丧中度过。只
要你的心没有停止跳动，一
切皆可重来。

HELP

Being helpful is about thinking about the public good
and being grateful. It is about always feeling love for
others. If you do not believe that this world is a world
of love, your life is mostly spent in depression. As
long as the heart is undefeated, everything can start
again.

欲望

欲望有合理和不合理之分。

如果合理，那么尽力去追求。有些欲望是不合理的。

人们不应该追求不合理的欲望，因为这样会损人不利己。认清自己想要什么很重要，但更重要的是，分清哪些是合理的，哪些不合理。

DESIRE

There are reasonable and unreasonable desires. The unreasonable ones should not be pursued as doing so will hurt yourself and others over time. It is important to understand what your desires are, but more important to know what are the reasonable and what are the unreasonable desires in your life.

遗憾

遗憾有很多种理解。你应该

能想到很多你一生中应该做

却没有做的事情。对于其中

一些事情，你可能还有时间

去做。然而有些事情，光阴

一去不复返，你需要接受不

能做的现实。生活中难免会

有遗憾，或小或大，要把注

意力集中在你做完的事情和

已取得的成就上，而不是你

还没有做的事情上。将遗憾

减少到最低。

REGRET

Regret can have a lot of meanings. You can think about many things you could have done or should have done in your life. For some there still may be time. For other things, the time has passed and you need to accept that. Your life will have some regrets, sometimes small and sometimes big, but focus on the things that you have done, things you have achieved, and not on the things that you have not accomplished. Regret is not a fruit we should harvest too often.

仪式

仪式文化非常重要。它赋予人们认知，传达思想，展示成就，它是从人生的一个位置到另一个位置的通道。仪式为所有参加者带来荣誉和快乐。

CEREMONY

The culture of ceremony is very important. It gives recognition, it conveys meaning, it shows achievement, it gives passage from one place to another in your life. Ceremony honors and brings happiness to all who take part.

谅解

谅解别人也就是善待自己。如果你与他人的关系存在冲突，那么你需要试着去谅解他们。尽自己最大的努力去谅解别人，同时永远记得谅解自己，并从错误中汲取教训。

FORGIVENESS

You need to forgive others and also to treat yourself well. If you are in a relationship with others and there is any conflict, then you need to try to forgive them. Do your best to forgive, and always remember to forgive yourself and learn from your mistakes.

平凡

人们有不同的标准，不同的需求，以及不同的行为方式。有些人甘于平凡，然而有些人却在生活中追求不同的标准，接触不同的人，建立不同的价值观。人们有时会选择成为前者或成为后者，但两者都是好的，都需要努力才能实现。重要的是，要知道自己想成为什么样的人以及想过怎样的生活。

ORDINARY

People have different standards, different needs and different ways. Someone can want to be ordinary and that is okay. Someone else may not want to be ordinary, to have different standards, different people in their life and different values in their life. People can sometimes choose to be one or the other, but either is okay and both take effort. It is important for people, however, to know what they want to be and how they want to live.

妥协

狭路相逢时，每个人都必须
适当让一步，能够让别人方
便通过。

慈善

我一心行善。我希望其他人
也尽可能去做力所能及的善
事。发自内心地给予别人或
点滴或重大的帮助，这是你
找到幸福的重要途径。

COMPROMISE

We are all on a narrow path, so every individual must be comfortable to step aside and allow others to pass.

CHARITY

I give from the heart. I hope others do the same to the extent that they are able to give. Giving a little, or a lot, from the heart is an important way to find happiness for yourself.

目标

很多人没有目标，或者经常改变目标。这些人往往是漫无目的，或总是对自己的生活不满足。人们需要找到或选择一个适合自己的目标。

一个能带给自己决心、动力和幸福感的目标。设定的目标应该是现实的、可实现的和长期的。

GOAL

Many people have no goal or they have many changing goals. These people will often be aimless or dissatisfied. People need to find or choose a goal that is right for them. Find a goal that gives purpose, motivation and happiness. Your goal should be realistic, achievable and long term.

你应该有目标，但最重要的
是朝着这个目标努力，而不
能纸上谈兵。为了达到目标
和梦想，你必须了解自己，
了解自己在每一步中哪些做
错了、哪些是对的，在此基
础上再进行下一步。这样就
可以不断学习和进步，实现
自己的梦想和目标。

You should know your goal, but the most important thing is the effort to work towards that goal. Just wishing and wanting does not let you achieve it. In order to achieve the goal and the dream you must know yourself, understand what you did wrong and what you did right at various steps, and on that basis move to the next step. That way you constantly learn and you always move closer to achieving your dream and your goal.

擬古

青松劲挺姿，凌霄恥
屈，览种出枝蘖，垂
连上松端秋花墅烽烟
蒋雄堂锦殷不华不
自立铎光射九之坤见
吐乎效鹤疑缩颓还
青松本无华，安得保
岁寒
龟鹤年寿齐羽介所
记诛种、是灵物相接
应形驱鹤有冲霄心宽
殷戈尾居以竹雨附、相
将上云微报沖慎亏语
一语随缕尘

《蜀素帖》（局部）◎宋◎米芾

米芾是中国书法史上的大家，这幅《蜀素帖》为传世之作。其中提到的「龟鹤」两种动物，在中国文化中是健康长寿的象征。

Song Dynasty
Mi Fu
Shu Su Tie

270.8 × 27.8cm (part)
Mi Fu is a great master in the history of Chinese calligraphy. This is one of his most famous works. It mentions tortoise and crane, in Chinese culture they represent health and longevity.

晚年幸福

我希望当我九十九岁再回头

看时，感受到的是幸福和感

恩，并已经在大多数事情上

取得成功。我希望那时我已

经实现了自我价值，并为社

会创造了价值和利益。

HAPPINESS WHEN OLD

When I'm 99 years old I hope that when I look back I will feel happiness, gratitude, and will have been successful in most things. I hope I will think I have achieved value, and brought value and benefit to the society.

牺牲

父母老了需要孩子的照顾，
而孩子小时候需要父母的照
顾。这些事情简单而重要，
对大多数人来说很容易，但
我却没有尽到这些责任。我
母亲去世时，我正在出差，
为了履行我对海外员工的承
诺。因为工作伙伴，我有时
不得不牺牲自己的家庭生
活。但如果你生命中有更大
的清晰的目标，这些付出和
牺牲是值得的。

SACRIFICE

Parents need the attention of their children during
their old age and children need the attention of their
parents when they're young. Those simple and important truths and responsibilities are easy for most people, but for me, some of those responsibilities had to
be sacrificed. When my mother passed away I was on
a business trip, fulfilling a promise I had made to staff
overseas. For the work family I have sometimes had
to sacrifice my own family life. But a sacrifice becomes
worthwhile and happiness is found when the greater
purpose is clear.

年轻人

年轻人能够而且必须比老年人更努力地工作。他们有精力，有热情，如果他们努力工作，就有能力过上更好的生活。他们是国家和世界未来的领导者。我们对年轻人寄予厚望，期待他们的改变和进步。我希望年轻人能树立目标，愿意为人民，为社会，为国家，为这个世界做些事情。如果他们能记住这些，那么每天要做的工作就变得清晰和简单了。

THE YOUNG

The young can and must work even harder than the old. They have the energy, the enthusiasm and the ability to lead great lives if they work hard. They are the future leaders of the country and the world. The young are our investment in everything we cherish, including change and progress. I hope that the young have a goal, a desire to improve things for people, for society, for country and for the world. If they all keep that in mind, then the things they should be doing each day become clearer and easier.

悔恨

不要让自己沉浸在悔恨中无法自拔。正视它，并从中汲取教训，然后继续前进。当我做出了错误的决定，或者我和别人说话时用的词太苛刻，反思时我会对自己的言行感到后悔。这也是我们自我完善的途径，但不要让悔恨持续下去。

HATE

Never let hate for yourself last. Feel it, learn from it and move on. Sometimes when I make a bad decision, or when I speak with other people and the words I use are too harsh, when I reflect on it I feel that I hate myself. But that is also how we improve ourselves, so don't let the hate last.

自私

失败始于自私、嫉妒和傲慢，
而成功则总是源自于全心全
意、集思广益和奉献社会。
那些心胸狭隘、只关心自己的
人，是无法实现梦想的。

SELFISHNESS

Failure begins with selfishness, jealousy and arrogance,
but success always comes from whole-heartedness,
comprehensiveness and social commitment. Those
who concentrate on the narrow view, on themselves,
are less able to achieve their dreams.

64

海洋

对许多人来说，海洋代表着宽阔无垠，无法跨越。但是总有伟大的人物能找到远渡重洋的方法。海洋不会大过梦想，梦想会带来幸福。

OCEAN

For many, the ocean represents the impossible, a vast greatness too big to cross. But great people always find ways to cross oceans. The ocean is never bigger than the dream, and the dream brings happiness.

65

慷慨

慷慨大方，就是敞开心扉，为社会做出贡献。慷慨付出的回报，就是生活在一个更美好的世界中。你越大方，你就越富有。你越吝啬，你就越活在自私的贫困之中。

GENEROUS

To be generous is to have an open heart for people and to contribute to the society. To be generous is to be rewarded for meeting your responsibility to want to live in a better world. The more generous you are, the richer you will be. The stingier you are, the more you will live in the poverty of selfishness.

East Han Dynasty
Bronze Galloping Horse Treading on a Flying Swallow

34.5 × 45 × 13cm
A miracle of ancient China's bronze art and technique, the horse is galloping through the sky, treading on a swallow which is looking up back in amazement. The sculpture is "perfectly balanced on the one hoof which rests without pressure on a flying swallow…with the head vividly expressing mettlesome vigor."

《马踏飞燕》（青铜器）◎ 东汉

这是中国古代青铜雕塑的奇迹。天马凌空奔驰，超越于飞燕之上，整体造型飘逸俊美，充满动感。雕塑以飞燕和马蹄轻巧的接触，完美地解决了平衡问题，是青铜雕塑美学与技术上的奇迹。

马

马不能后退，它总是在前进。它是一种具备速度、耐力和方向感的动物，无论是个体还是群体，都能以力量和优雅的姿态立足。我们可以从马身上，学习感悟到很多有关力量、幸福和成功的东西。

HORSE

A horse cannot run backwards, it will always advance. It is an animal of speed, stamina and direction, and can cover ground with power and grace whether alone or in a group. From the horse we can learn much about strength, happiness and success.

第三部

财富

III

FORTUNE

尊重

在生活中，在事业上，做任
何事都要公平。这样才能赢
得尊重。如果你尊重别人，
别人也会尊重你，如果你想
要别人尊重你，却又不以公
平或者尊重别人的方式做
事，那么你也得不到尊重。
想要被尊重其实很简单，你
需要尊重他人，公平对待。

RESPECT

When you do anything in life or business, you need
to do it with fairness. That is how you gain respect. If
you give respect, then you are given respect. If you ex-
pect respect, but do not do things in a way that is fair
to or that respects others, then you will not be given
respect. Very simple really, to be honored with respect,
you need to be fair and show respect to others.

创新

创新是企业发展的源动力。它意味着不断挑战自我，意味着超越边界，超越现有框架，提升到一个新的境界。在经营企业时，你需要看到比企业现状更远的地方，站在更高的位置和视角。你需要面俱到、事事理清。当然，创新应以市场为导向。如果你的创新不能满足市场需求，或者不符合社会需要，那就没有意义了。创新必须立足于它所处的环境与背景才能成功。

INNOVATION

Innovation is the driving force of enterprise development. Innovation means to challenge yourself constantly. It means going into a new frontier, beyond borders, beyond the existing framework. If you have a business, you need to look beyond what the company is currently doing for a higher point of view and a higher position. You need to be able to look around and see clearly. However, innovation should be market oriented. If your innovation does not meet the demand of the market or if it does not meet a social need, then it is not meaningful. Innovation must be connected to its setting and context to succeed.

贫穷

贫穷是暂时的。关键在于你的心态和精神。贫穷没什么可怕的。相反，你应该害怕的是缺乏自信、懒惰和道德败坏。贫穷是一时的。如果你能改变心态，如果你是一个勤奋且富有创新精神的人，你迟早会摆脱贫困。

POVERTY

Poverty is temporary. The key is your mentality and energy. Poverty is nothing to be scared of. Instead, you should be afraid of lack of confidence, laziness and bad morals. Poverty itself is not the end. If you are able to change your mentality, if you are a hard worker and have an innovative spirit, sooner or later you will be out of poverty.

能量

能量来自梦想。如果你有梦想，那么你就有能量和信心。如果你有信心，你就不会低估自己。这本身就是能量。更大的能量来自行善和感恩，以及人们看待你对待你的方式。行善会给予你能量。

POWER

Power comes from dreams. If you have dreams, then you have power and confidence. If you have confidence, then you do not underestimate yourself. That, in itself, is power. Even greater power will then come from kindness of heart and from being grateful. Power is found in the way that others think about you and treat you. Kindness will give you power.

逆境

在我的商业生涯中，很多人试图向我们施加压力，操控我们，掠夺财富。有时企业几乎遭受毁灭性的打击。但最终，我们都挺过来了，因为我们心怀感激。我感谢那些让我们陷入困境的人。没有这些让我们痛苦并试图操控我们的人，我们就不会成长。我们感谢他们，因为他们是我们的『生命导师』。在他们的『磨难教导』下，我们变得百折不挠。

ADVERSITY

During my years in business a lot of people have tried to control us, take money from us and put pressure on us. Some moments have almost been catastrophic for the business. But in the end we won because of our grateful spirit. I am grateful to those who troubled us. Without the people who made us suffer and tried to control us, we would not grow. We are grateful to them as they are our life teachers. We are more resilient as a result of their teaching.

金钱

钱，我们生不带来，死不带去。钱是个好东西，但我又能吃多少、喝多少？我的饮食很普通，因为我需要营养，但也就仅此而已。金钱之外，每个人都有无尽的财富，那就是爱心。当你付出爱时，你会觉得世界更加美好。金钱永远不会给人那种感觉。

MONEY

We are born and we die without money. Money is good, but how much can I eat and drink? My meal is common because I need nourishment and nothing more. Regardless of money, all people have inexhaustible wealth in the form of love for others. When you pay with love, you feel the world is even more beautiful. Money can never give that feeling.

成功

成功源于自我努力、辛勤工
作、目标明确，以及帮助他
人。我希望别人也能通过这
些方式获得成功。重要的是
我们要记住，想要成功，想
要实现目标，首先需要与人
为善，相处融洽。

SUCCESS

Success comes from effort, working hard, knowing
your goals and supporting others. I hope that others
find success in these ways. It is important for us all to
remember that to be successful, to achieve a goal, the
first thing needed is to get along with people well.

努力

个人努力在所有事情中至关重要。有时它很难，需要克服诸多障碍。但只有通过努力，包括精神和身体两方面的努力，我们才能达到目标。当然，个人的努力还不够，你还需要那些具备你所没有的天赋的人，需要他们与你共同努力来实现你的目标。

EFFORT

Personal effort is essential in all things. Sometimes it can be very hard and sometimes many obstacles need to be dealt with. But only through effort, both mental and physical, can we achieve our goals. And effort cannot occur alone, you need other people who have talents that you do not have and who are willing to use their effort with yours to achieve together.

命运

这很重要。你需要付出努力，建立良好的基础，好运也会随之而来。幸运总是青睐努力力的人。

勇敢

在你做一些公平有益的、对社会有所贡献的事情时，你会变得勇敢。所谓勇敢，就是用你的思想、你的心灵、你的双手为社会做出贡献。

FATE

This is very important. You need to make effort by yourself, work hard to build good foundations, and good fate will come afterwards. Good fate follows from strong effort.

BRAVERY

When you do something that is fair, that contributes to the society, then you are being brave. Contributing to society with your mind, your heart and your hands is what bravery is about.

有人逃避挑战，有人把它看作机会。困难和挑战是生活的一部分，或大或小。挑战本身并不重要，重要的是我们如何看待它和解决它。我们如何应对挑战将决定我们成为什么样的人，决定我们能否克服面临的挑战和困难。

挑战

CHALLENGE

Some people run away from challenges, while others see them as opportunities. Difficulties and challenges are part of life, sometimes big and sometimes small. It is not important what the challenge is, what is important is how we see it and how we approach it. How we deal with a challenge is what defines us as human beings, and is what determines whether we will overcome the challenge or difficulty that we are facing.

财富

财富是一种责任。有些有钱人花钱只是为了享乐，为了自己，也许还有其他少数人。但对我来说，我觉得拥有的财富越多，所要承担的社会责任就越多。你花钱的目的，应当是帮助他人找到健康和财富，帮助那些因处境而缺少机遇的人。财富的真正价值和乐趣，是利用它给他人带来改变，而不仅仅是浪费在自己身上。真正的幸福是帮助他人，履行社会责任。

WEALTH

Wealth is a responsibility. Some people with wealth just use it for enjoyment, for themselves and perhaps a few others. For me, though, I think the more you have wealth, the more you have social responsibility. You must use that wealth for a purpose, to help others find health and to find wealth themselves. You should also help others who because of their situation have less opportunities. The real value and enjoyment of wealth is using it to make a difference for others, not just wasting it on yourself. True happiness is in helping others and meeting the responsibilities of having wealth.

团队

团队既是一种管理体系，也是一种精神体系，二者共同推动目标的实现。有共同的目标，团结奋斗，公平回报，互相尊重、互相欣赏，才是一个能有效运作、做好事情的优秀团队。

领导力

领导力是一门艺术。个人价值观、自信和向他人展示自己的方式，都会逐步建立你的领导力。

TEAM

The team is a system of management and spirit that comes together to promote an outcome. Sharing a purpose, working hard, coming together, being rewarded together fairly and respecting and enjoying each other all mean that a good team will work well together to do good things.

LEADERSHIP

Leadership is an art of being. Personal values, confidence and the way in which you present yourself to others all build up your leadership.

历史

历史可以是个人的历史，也可以是一个民族的历史，一个国家的历史，世界的历史。我们能从历史中学到很多。古代传统文化形成了我个人的历史背景和我们国家的历史背景。古代文化的影响随处可见，尽管不是每个人都能认识到这种影响的根源。我们也正在创造历史，它将影响未来的人们。我们都是历史长河的一部分，这条历史河流曾向我们，也终将流经我们继续向前。

HISTORY

History can mean personal history, the history of a people, of a country, of the world. But we can learn a lot from the ancient history. The ancient culture has formed my background and the background of my country. The influence of the ancient culture can be seen everywhere, even though not everyone will recognize the roots of the influence. And we are creating history now that will influence the people of future time. We are all part of the river of history, the river that flowed before us and will flow after us as well.

知者知家丹牛未爛漫蕉葉倒蒼苔漫伊遮盖

藤鹽墨免倩隣首抹冤腮 青藤道士徐渭

《蕉石牡丹图》◎ 明 ◎ 徐渭

一反过去中国写意花鸟画恬静安适的意趣，徐渭赋予笔下的花卉以强烈的主观情感，产生强烈的艺术感染力。

Ming Dynasty, Xu Wei, **Palm, Stone and Peony**

195 × 99cm

Xu Wei adds a strong personal and emotional touch to his paintings, which made his works a major challenge to the tradition of Chinese paintings that advocate peace, harmony and tranquility.

做出决定就要承担责任。领导者应该善于决策，因为那些擅长于此的人将获得团队的尊重。那些没有勇气做出决定、不能做出正确及时决策的人，不会是好的领导。

决定

DECISION

To make a decision is to take responsibility. Leaders should be good at decision making because those who are good at this will gain the respect of their teams. Those who do not have the courage to make decisions and cannot make correct and timely decisions will not be good leaders.

腐败

腐败是可耻的。它的存在令
人难堪。在一个良好而公平
的社会里，没有必要腐败。
即使有些人被诱惑，他们周
围的社会及他人，都应该态
度明确：腐败是不对的。腐
败不应成为任何人想要追求
的生活方式。

CORRUPTION

It is a shame that corruption exists. It embarrasses us
all for it to exist. In a good and fair society there is no
need for corruption. Even if some people are tempted
to be corrupt, the society around them and all the
other people should make it clear that it is not right
to be corrupt. It is not the way that anyone wants life
to be.

龙

龙是皇帝的象征，是中国文化的重要符号，它能凝聚人心，让人们为共同的事业齐心协力。

DRAGON

The dragon is a symbol of the Emperor. It is a very important icon of the Chinese culture. It helps bring people together and keeps people focused on the things that matter to us all.

动力

想要有动力，就要有梦想，有目标，并追求这个目标。

要想拥有并保持生活的动力，你需要设定一个你想要做的或者想要实现的目标。

你必须明确你为之奋斗的方向。否则你就不会有动力，你会漫无目的，或者在各种事务之间不停转移目标。

MOTIVATION

To be motivated is to have a dream, to have a purpose, to pursue that purpose. To have and to keep motivation in life, you need to set a goal, a target, what you want to do or achieve. You have to know where you are going to stay truly motivated. If you don't have this, you won't be motivated in life, you will be aimless or you will drift from one thing to another without real interest or real commitment.

前进

要开始新的事物，走一条不同的道路，你必须勇敢。但与此同时，要做到这一点，你需要放弃一些东西。因此，在人生中我们会挑选那些有价值、有意义的东西，放弃那些毫无价值的东西。你需要选择该选择的，放弃该放弃的。一旦做出决定，就应毫不犹豫。

ADVANCE

To start something new, to advance down a different path, you have to be daring. But at the same time, to achieve this you need to give something up. So in life we pick things up that come with value and that come with meaning and we give things up that are worthless. You need to choose the right thing to pick up and you need to choose the right thing to give up. When you make the decision, you should not hesitate.

另一个重要的问题是，你决不能脚踏两条船，否则你就会掉进水里。向前走，永远不要为自己留后路。一旦你知道自己有后路可走，你就难以专注于一往无前的道路。

Another important point is that you should never put two feet on two different boats. Stick to one, or else you will fall into the water. Move forward and never reserve a way back for yourself. Once you know you have a backup plan, it will stop you from dedicating yourself to the way forward.

时间

生命、工作和机遇都是可以用来体现时间价值的重要元素。有些东西在生命中是独一无二的，它们只发生一次或只在那一瞬间。很多人和事情，一旦错过就不再来。时光易逝永不回，我们必须珍惜时间。

TIME

Life, work and opportunities all represent time, a major, important element. Some things are unique in life, they happen only for one time or for a short time. If you miss those things, then time moves on and you cannot go back to those things. Once passed time cannot come back. We must all cherish time and understand that it passes all too quickly.

不可能

不可能能被完成。不可能能成为可能。困难只是毛毛雨，不是暴风雨。细雨阻止不了人们前进。

斗牛士

生活中，我们应当像一个斗牛士。接受挑战，面对挑战，不畏惧挑战。坚守阵地，必要时稍作调整，但始终把你的目光、你的心思专注于成功上。

IMPOSSIBLE

Impossible can be accomplished. Impossible can become possible. Difficulties are just drizzle, they are not a storm. Drizzle never stopped anybody from moving forward.

BULLFIGHTER

In much of life we must be like a bullfighter. Accept challenge. Face challenge. Do not be afraid of challenge. Stand your ground, move a little when needed, but keep your eyes, your mind and your heart on success.

道路

路是人走出来的。你不前
进，就不能开辟道路。就生
活中的大多数事情来说，在
你迈进之前，并不存在明确
的途径。随着你向前迈进，
你开辟出了道路，然后进一
步前行。

PATHWAY

Humans create pathways as they move forward. If you
are not moving forward, then you are not creating a
pathway. For most things in life a clear pathway does
not exist before you move forward. As you move
forward, you create the pathway which then allows
you to move forward further.

随着中国过去三十年经济的不断变革，政府和人民观念的改变，中国在不断进步。在此之前，中国是一头沉睡的雄狮。现在，它被唤醒了，成为世界经济和社会的中坚力量。

中国

CHINA

China continues to rise because of the past 30 years of economic reform and because of the worldview of the government and the people. Before that, China was a sleeping lion. Now it has woken up as an economic and social power.

文明

文明和文化是相连的，二者在同步发展。我们有责任促成、理解、感激那些帮助我们持续朝着和谐统一美好社会前进的文明和文化的变化。

CIVILIZATION

Civilization and culture are linked. As one develops, so does the other. We have a responsibility to contribute, to understand and to appreciate the changes in civilization and in culture that help us all to keep moving forward to a better society of harmony and unity.

遗产

人生不带来死不带去。人的一生，应该为社会作贡献，这是我们所有人的责任，也是我们的荣幸。如果当我们离开时，人们能够记住我们，那才是我们留下的真正遗产。我们可能会留下其他东西，但最重要的遗产，是在我们离开之后，人们对我们的情感和看法。被看作是一个对他人和社会有所贡献的好人，是最重要的遗产。

LEGACY

People are born and they die without anything. During your lifetime you have to contribute to society, that is the responsibility and the privilege of all of us to contribute. How people remember us when we are gone is the real legacy that we leave. We might leave other things, but it is the feelings and thoughts that people have about us after we have gone that is the most important legacy. Being thought of as a good person who contributed to others and to society is the most important legacy.

机会

无论你做什么，机会都是少有且珍贵的。有机会给你，这很宝贵。就我自己的经验而言，你一辈子也不会有很多机会，因此，一旦你有机会，一旦你看到了机会，你就应该牢牢抓住它。

OPPORTUNITY

Whatever you do, opportunity is very rare and very precious. It is very precious to have opportunity available to you. Based on my own experience, you do not have a lot of opportunities in your life, so if you have an opportunity, if you can see an opportunity in any part of your life, then you should grasp it.

选择

当你做出了正确的选择，不
要犹豫，不要怀疑。正确的
决定其实很简单。为了确
保你做出正确的决定，你必
须看到事情背后的真相，而
不是流于表面。你做出的决
定，应当有益于人民，有益
于企业，有益于社会。正确
的决策背后是基于强大的道
德观。

CHOICE

When you are making the right choice there is no
hesitation and no doubt. Therefore, the right decision
is actually very straightforward. To make sure you are
making the right decision you have to look for the
truth behind the facts rather than simply looking at
what is on the surface. The decision you make must
bring benefits to people, business and society. Behind
a good decision is strong morality.

才能

我们所说的才能，是指一个人为社会作贡献、创造利益的能力。但才能的发挥需要信任。如果你信赖某人，你就给他展示才能的空间。把合适的人放在合适的位置，他们就能做好任何工作。

TALENT

When we talk about talent, we talk about ability and capability, meaning a person can really contribute to the society and bring benefit. But talent is also about mutual trust. If you trust somebody, you give them space to contribute and to show their own talents and capabilities. If you put the right person in the right place they can achieve anything.

工作

工作是多层次的责任。它是你达成目标的途径，也是你养家糊口、建立友谊、维持你的公司、支持你的国家的方式。

传统

传统会随着社会的进步而发展改变。传统应当被尊重，但也要与时俱进。

WORK

Work is responsibility on many levels. It is a way to get to what you want to achieve, to get to a goal. It is a way of supporting your family, creating friendships, and supporting your company and your country.

TRADITION

Tradition evolves with social progress. When society improves, then tradition follows too. Traditions must be respected, but they also must change to match the time and the people of that time.

非凡

我要做什么事时，总是试图创造一些不同的东西，不同于以往我做过的，也不同于别人做过的。做非凡的事情，就是创造能给许多人带来巨大快乐的一个个小的奇迹。

公司

企业小的时候是个人的，发展起来后，是国家的，是大家的，是社会的。它为社会大众的利益而存在。

EXTRAORDINARY

When I do something, I always try to create something that is different, that is extra to what I've done before and to what others have done before. To do something extraordinary is to create a small miracle that brings great joy to many.

COMPANY

When the company is small, it is personal. It belongs to the founder. When it is large and successful, it belongs to its staff and to its country. It exists for the social good.

执行

在执行过程中，把一个重大的、长期的目标分解成一个个可实现的短期目标，然后一个一个完成，这很重要。那些眼里只有长期目标的人往往根本不采取行动，因此他们失败了。当你接一个地完成小目标时，大的目标自然就会实现。因此，在制定小目标中，不要好高骛远，永远保持实际。人们认为成功来自于尝试不可能的事情，恰恰相反，它通常来自于踏实和效率。

EXECUTION

In the process of execution, breaking a major, long-term goal into achievable, short-term actions, then completing them one by one is of great importance. Those who only focus on the long-term goal often take no action at all, therefore they fail. When you complete small goals one by one, the large goal will be achieved naturally. So in your smaller goals, don't over-stretch, don't be over-ambitious, and always remain practical. People think success comes from attempting the impossible but, on the contrary, it is about modesty and efficiency.

《墨葡萄图》◎ 明 ◎ 徐渭

徐渭是明代书画和诗词大家。他为人狂放不羁，他的画同样惊世骇俗，打破了传统的手法、题材范畴和审美规范，自成一家。

这幅《墨葡萄图》风格疏放，不求形似，代表了徐渭大写意花卉的风格，也是明代写意花卉高水平的杰作。

Ming Dynasty, Xu Wei, **Grapes**

116.4 × 64.3cm

Xu Wei is one of the great painters of ancient China. Like his own character, his painting is so full of life and unrestrained that he created a genre of his own, "Green Vine" which opened the gate to Chinese modern painting. This is a masterpiece of Xu Wei, which represents the highest level of freehand Chinese painting.

一线

有多少高级管理人员定期到一线探访？又有多少人了解员工面临的实际问题，并提出切实可行的解决方案？有多少经理让一线员工了解他的战略目标和管理理念，并对每个职位的职能有深刻的了解？又有多少经理亲自指导、激励和表扬他们的一线员工？公司的重要决策需要在一线落实，一个不经常探访一线，不了解来自一线的独特变化和挑战的经理，无法为他们的业务做出正确的决策。

FRONTLINE

How many senior managers regularly visit the frontline? How many recognize real problems being faced by their staff and come up with practical solutions? How many managers broadcast to their frontline staff their strategic targets and management philosophies, and have a deep understanding of the tasks and responsibilities of each and every position? How many managers coach, motivate and praise their frontline staff in person? The frontline is where the single most important actions occur for any company. A manager who does not regularly visit and who does not understand the unique changes and challenges coming from the frontline is not going to make the right decisions for their business.

管理

管理者必须懂得如何与人真诚相处。真诚和真实能温暖人心，创造一种人人都能诚意行事的环境。这是个人和企业发展的绝佳氛围。一个真正可靠的人，更多的是理解和肯定，而非一味批评。这样的人不会冷漠，拒人于千里之外，而是热心、善于鼓舞士气的人。

MANAGEMENT

Managers must know how to act in a genuine manner around other people. Being genuine and authentic will warm many hearts and create an environment in which everybody is comfortable to act sincerely. This is an excellent atmosphere for personal and business development. A truly authentic person is less critical and more understanding and positive. They are not cold and do not deal with people at arm's length, but instead they are warm-hearted and encouraging.

竞争

商业竞争是血腥残酷的。这场比赛中唯一的规则就是丛林法则——适者生存。优胜者获得奖赏，而弱者消失。狭路相逢，妥协意味着彼此各自让步，而竞争是将你的对手打倒出局。在竞争激烈的环境中，只有最勇敢的人才能胜出。获得竞争胜利的企业，也应为能够继续向员工提供稳定的工作和职业发展而感恩。

COMPETITION

Competition in business is bloody and cruel. The only rule in this competition is the law of the jungle – survival of the fittest. It rewards the superior and eliminates the weak. Compromise involves stepping aside for one another on a narrow path, but competition is about knocking your opponent off that path. In an environment of fierce competition, only the bravest can win. The victorious business should be grateful for the fact that it can continue to offer job security and career advancement to its people.

成就梦想：李金元语录
© 2017 by 李金元，凯文·麦康基
所有权利保留

ISBN 10: 0-9994263-2-X
ISBN 13: 978-0-9994263-2-6

2017 壹嘉出版
装帧设计：视觉共振设计工作室

www.1plusbooks.com
旧金山，美国

Achieving Your Dream: Words from Li Jinyuan
© 2017 by Li Jinyuan, Kevin McConkey
All Rights Reserved

ISBN 10: 0-9994263-2-X
ISBN 13: 978-0-9994263-2-6

2017 1 Plus Books
Published in the United States
Book design by PanGo Vision

www.1plusbooks.com
San Francisco, USA